one and all

IAN COOPER

One and All

A Spiritual Perspective on Getting Along

To Meg, Jo and Tim; my champions

"Love everyone and tell the truth."

—Neem Karoli Baba

Contents

Preface   ii

Acknowledgement   v

1   Let's start with the truth   1

2   There is no self   5

3   We don't know   12

4   Don't take any of it too seriously   17

5   We're stuck   22

6   We are the mud and the lotus   29

7   Action and acceptance   35

8   Taking a good look at ourselves   40

9   Being no one   46

10 What can we do to help?   50

11 Come on in   53

12 Unity through diversity   57

13 A brief meditation   63

14 Every meeting is sacred   65

15 What does justice look like?   71

16 Loving the stranger   76

17 A call to action   79

Afterword   81

About the Author   84

Preface

While this book aims to transcend a particular place and time, it has certainly been inspired by one. Those of us living in the United States have been taking quite a ride these past few years. As I write, we continue to experience the effects of a once-in-a-century public health crisis and a blend of political, racial, and cultural tensions unlike any in living memory.

This book is not about either. But it is about what we can do to salve the long-standing wounds in our community that have been laid bare. The division among us is plain to see, but how do we bridge the gaps and reconcile?

The need to come together isn't just confined to America, of course. The world over, there is a hunger for freedom, equality, and justice. Many of us look at the future of our planet and see it balanced on the edge of a knife. We feel unsteady and we know that something must be done. But what?

What we need is to find a way to love each other and to get along. That's a big task, and I won't pretend to have the journey all mapped out. But I know where we can start. Mystics and spiritual teachers from all traditions tell us that we are one with each other and the universe as a whole. All of our divisions, in other words, are illusions. When we start to dive into and live from that beautiful truth, we plant the seeds for a free and loving community for one and all.

If universal oneness seems at odds with how we see things,

that's okay. If we are patient, honest, and pay attention to our intuition, we will find that our hearts know it to be true. Truth belongs to no one and exists in all of us. My goal here is simply to offer a reminder of what we all already know.

To move forward towards seeing our inherent unity, we need to soften to each other. In order to do that, in a deep, meaningful way, we need to take an honest look inside ourselves. We need to say yes to what we see (all of it), turn our gaze toward our inner sense of universal love and truth, and then act from that place.

Looking inside ourselves is important because the more clearly we see ourselves, the more we will intuitively know how to get along better with our fellows. Why? Because we will start to connect with our wisdom, nurture our compassion, and recognize ourselves in each other.

The road is bumpy, but we can take heart. It's all part of the process: our differences, our confusion, and our pain exist to encourage us to search for the deeper unity within. When we do, we start to see that the kind of world we all want to live in comes from that spirit of oneness inside us.

All of us have a part to play here. We each have our own path to walk, but we all have the power to embody the divine and to light up the earth. If we truly want to be at ease in ourselves, be at peace with each other, and let freedom ring across the world, now is a good time to start.

This book is an attempt to contribute to that effort. It draws from several spiritual traditions but isn't wedded to any one in particular. Don't take any of it too seriously. I hope it rings true.

Thanks for being here,

Ian Cooper

Los Angeles, California, February 2021

Acknowledgement

I want to share my gratitude for everyone who helped me in creating this book. Thank you to Tim and Jo for their tireless support and help editing; to Ed and Barb for their generosity beyond reason; to Anh and Gene for taking the time to read and offer feedback; to Max for wanting to hear what I have to say; and to Pamela and Norman, for their wisdom, kindness, and guidance. Special thanks to Zack for never thinking that I'm too far out, encouraging me throughout the creative process, and helping carry the manuscript over the finish line. I also want to honor all of the other friends, past and present, who have supported me along the road of awakening and recovery that kicked this all off so many years ago. Each and every one of you is in these pages.

Most of all, thank you to my wife Meg, who not only helped me edit (and came up with the title), but believed that I had a book in me long before I ever started taking the prospect seriously myself. This one does not exist without her.

1

Let's start with the truth

We all want to love each other. That is our natural state of being. Sure, many of us spend a great deal of time pretending otherwise, but that's only because we've gotten lost along the way.

When we get too far off track, though, conflict and division start to spring up among us. If we look around at our community today, we probably see a good deal of that. There is a hard rain falling down on us. Disagreements, differences of opinion, even fighting: these are all part of the human experience. But when our conflicts fester and we start to see each other as less than human and lose track of our love for one another, then we're in for trouble.

So, when we see conflict in our society, what can we do to help? When we find ourselves struggling to get along with those around us, how do we set things right? What do we need to do to come together as a community and love one another?

That is a big question. But it is as current, vital, and urgent as any we can ask, save, perhaps, "What's for dinner?" It is a question that invites us to examine our deepest sense of who and what we are, and in doing so, gives us an opportunity to shake up the world and usher in the new. Our struggle to get along, especially today, when the world feels smaller than ever and escape grows ever more difficult, is challenging us to return to that natural state of loving one another. We can't get away from each other—not really, anyway—so what other choice do we have?

Building a peaceful, loving community for all of us (for all people, all beings, everywhere) means working together across all aspects of society: governments, businesses, houses of worship, community groups, and families. That kind of cooperation, however, is not where we begin the process of coming together. Our starting point (and the focus of this book) is very simple: we want to get to know the truth that is inside of all of us, right here and right now. No matter how bad things are, there is good news: a willingness to explore the truth is all that we need in order to start healing the wounds that tear us apart.

This means that all of us can help. We don't need to be anyone in particular. It doesn't matter what we believe or what we know or what our lives look like. All we have to do is be willing to take a look inside ourselves and act to serve our community as a whole. Each of us has a part to play in bringing us all together.

In this book, we'll talk about a few different perspectives and practices that can help us to do that. There are many others as well! One of the beautiful things about our journey into truth is that we each have our own path and get to go at our own pace. We get to find our own way forward because we're journeying into ourselves. But the truth at the center that we're all moving towards is this: everyone, everywhere, is us. There is no one else, because none of us are separate from the rest of us.

This might feel like an obvious thing to say, and it is! We

all know the truth, remember? But how many of us actually live this way? How many of us feel it? Sure, yeah, we care, but we get caught up in our divisions real quick. We divide the world into us and them without even noticing that we're doing it, because what else would we do? How else would we know where we stand? Who are we without someone to define ourselves against?

Well, maybe we don't need to stand anywhere or be anyone specific. Besides, the truth we're talking about here goes deeper than just the fact that we all share the same earth. Yeah, that's a part of it, but only a small part. The bigger part is that we are totally, completely connected to each other and to the universe as a whole. There is no us and them, no me and you. Not really. There is only one of us, infinite, unified. This is the being (and we could even use a capital B) from which we come and shall one day return; the Being that right here and now, is also totally, completely what we are. We all want to love each other because we are each other.

Thich Nhat Hanh describes the nature of reality as *inter-being*. What he means is that we're not independent but interdependent, at even the most basic, elemental level. We *inter-are*: none of us can exist without the rest of us. Even the mighty redwood tree cannot grow without the seed, the rain, the soil, and all of the little creatures that help nurture the health of the forest simply by being. Nothing can be removed from the whole. There is room for all of us.

If this is starting to feel like a lot to wrap our heads around, yes. Our heads are only going to get us so far here (more on that to come). That's okay. We don't have to have anything figured out right now, or ever, for that matter. Our sense of oneness may get buried, but on some level, our hearts know the truth.

3

That's more than enough to start.

2

There is no self

So, what we've begun to talk about is the nature of the self. What, exactly, is that? Who, what, are we?

That's a great question to ask. We have to be someone, right? After all, that's how we probably relate to everything around us: as a separate self. We think of ourselves as an individual moving through the world, making decisions, taking actions, chasing goals, in charge of our lives (or at least trying to be). Adyashanti describes the self as more of a habit than anything else, but for most of us, our sense of being someone feels solid, serious, and real. But is it?

No. Not really, anyway. We don't exist independent of the present moment. What we think of as an individual self is just one ever-changing face of the entire universe. No-self, the Buddha calls it. He tells us that there is nothing in us that we can hold on to—that we are empty. Who we are is entirely at the mercy of what is.

What does it mean to be empty? Everything and nothing. But, a piece of emptiness is that none of our identities or experiences are permanent. There is no part of ourselves that we can point to and say, "This is the real me." Yeah, we all believe that we're somebody, but then we then wake up one morning and see that we're no longer that person. The caterpillar becomes a chrysalis that grows into a butterfly. Despite our best efforts, we always change. No form or shape ever stays the same: not just bodies, but thoughts, perceptions, feelings, and even consciousness itself.

This may all sound abstract, but no-self, emptiness, is actually what is going on right here and now. One way we can start getting acquainted is by noticing when we feel like we're not enough or are missing something inside us. Yes! That's not a flaw, but the nature of reality poking through. Sure, most of us try to build ourselves up in response to that feeling, but we never quite succeed, do we? Why? Because we can never fully be anyone in particular or separate ourselves from the whole. Nothing ever settles.

We can borrow a line from the poet Rumi and think of the self as a mirage in the desert. Most of us spend our lives chasing the illusion, trying to make ourselves into the person we want to be. Like a sun-baked traveler craving a drink of cool water and a little shade, we imagine that surely we must be on the cusp of getting there. Just work hard enough, right? One more step and we're home. But no matter how hard we try, we always remain one step away. The dream of self hovers just outside our grasp.

The notion that we don't have a self is a lot to take in, and we'll talk more about it as the book goes on. It may sound a little scary, too, especially if we're used to running away from our innate awareness of emptiness. Who among us isn't at least a little afraid of the void? So let's have fun for a moment, and explore the flip-side of no-self. Here's the thing: if none of us are actually separate from the whole, then the whole universe is us. To be empty is to be full.

Ramana Maharshi, teaching from his cave on the slopes of the Arunachala mountain, puts it like this: that everything is self—one, single Self shared by all. We don't each have our own little corner of the kingdom, and that means the whole thing is ours! All-Self, we could call it. If none of us can ever be fully individual, then there is only one of us, inter-being: God, Allah, within us all. Underneath the ever-changing forms, we're not just one, but the same. When Christ tells us to love our neighbors as ourselves, he is taking this truth to its practical conclusion.

Is Ramana contradicting what the Buddha tells us? Yes! No! There is no one right way to talk about any of this stuff. But both teachers are urging us to remember that we each have the power to see the unity of all things and witness the lines that seem to divide the world fall away before our eyes. Where does the individual stop and the community start? That boundary doesn't exist. It's all just one continuous dance. God is empty and so are we.

If we want to put this in more ordinary language, we can also just say that nothing is personal. Everything about us is simply what's happening. All of our identities are only costumes. We wear them for a while and then cast them aside. Take a good enough look and even the most fundamental building blocks of self, like gender or ethnicity, will crumble to dust. Are we ever really the same person twice? No! Do we have deeply held beliefs? Doubt is coming! We can't stand on any of it. All those parts of ourselves that we think make us us are like clouds passing in the sky. Here one moment and gone the next. Can we hold on to a cloud or push it away? Of course not.

If nothing is personal, then everything is okay. We can go ahead and accept all of it: our thoughts, feelings, experiences, and the emptiness from which it all comes. We don't have to reject any aspect of the present moment or lie to ourselves about anything. We don't even have to try and force ourselves to understand emptiness: the mirage of having a self is just another part of what's happening now. We can be with all of it, say yes to all of it, but we don't have to take any of it personally (or too seriously, for that matter). The more we accept what is, right here and right now, the less of a hold anything has on us.

At this point, we might think, "None it is personal and the whole universe is ours? Tell that to my landlord when the rent comes due." Fair enough. But that, too, is part of the truth. We're not plumbing the depths of reality to get out of living in the world, but so that we can show up for all of it and for all of us. Indeed, part of accepting what is means saying yes to what's in front of us—including all the mess of everyday living—and helping out. Because we're not separate, what we do affects the whole community. Our every action ripples out into the world like the waves from a stone skipped across the surface of a pond.

That landlord is actually just one more reminder that we inter-are. We can't ever get away from the rest of us. There is nowhere to run. Yeah, we can try to meditate (or drink) ourselves into another plane of consciousness, but no matter how hard we try, eventually, we'll get hungry and need to eat. Every aspect of our experience may be passing clouds, but the morning rain still soaks us to the bone. No-self, God, emptiness: these are not ideals but words that point towards the practical, ordinary truth that lives within us all.

If we want to start getting to know the truth, there is only one place to look: inside ourselves, within our bodies, here and now. Yeah, we don't have a self, but that's okay, because truth, God, emptiness—that's the real us. All of us are unconditional love and universal wisdom dressed up in a billion different forms. To see this, we just have to turn our gaze inwards and start paying attention.

We have to look for truth inside ourselves because just hearing about it isn't enough. The heart of truth can't be put into words or understood by reading a book. It's not about smart. It's more intimate than that. Truth is about getting to know ourselves, and by grounding ourselves in the here and now, we open to the truth. We can't put it into words or write it down, but that's okay. What we can do is be the truth; be empty; be God; be. Not so bad, right?

Focusing our search for truth on the here and now also reminds us not to forget about what's going on inside of us and in front of us. None of us can float up in the sky forever. No matter how much we try to zen out or how many drugs we take, we can't get away from our bodies. What goes up must come down. Why? Because our bodies are the truth. We're vulnerable and always-changing. When we're tired, we need rest. Even if we've got a shelf full of spiritual books beside our bed.

If we have needs, well, those around us do too. Indeed, what does all of this mean for the community as a whole? Well, the same truth applies. The community is our collective body, and just like each of us, the community isn't solid. Our group experiences, our group narratives, the institutions and structures that make up our society, none of it is permanent or, ultimately, real. The community is empty too.

But, still, the landlord comes for us all. We're all still here, trying to make it from one end of the day to the other. When we see someone sleeping on a street corner, what we're really seeing is us in a different form. When we greet a neighbor or work with a client or have lunch with a friend, we're meeting with ourselves. If none of it is personal to any of us, then we are each all of it. There's no one else left.

This can take us to some radical conclusions about how to shape our society. After all, our priorities change if we start to understand that the people we don't care about or even hate *are us*. Getting along, sharing, helping out; these become less altruistic and more acts of practical self-interest.

"Treat everyone you meet like God in drag," Ram Dass says. The God he's talking about isn't an old man in the sky or a grumpy judge on a high seat. Ram Dass's God, our God, is the unconditionally loving reality within us all. Each and every one of us is perfect, complete, whole. In the Bhagavad Gita, when God appears as Krishna and shows us that he holds the entire universe inside himself, the punchline is that we are each actually Krishna. We might think of ourselves as a man or a woman, husband or a wife, a member of a tribe, a friend, a lover, whatever, but we're all just God playing with God.

But how many of us see that? More importantly, how many of us allow ourselves to feel that? Really feel it, in our bones? Not so many, right? That's what the game is about then. That's what being part of the community is about. Day by day, year by year, breath by breath, we can remember that everyone we meet, whether for a moment or for a lifetime, is us and act accordingly. When Christ reminds us to treat others as we would be treated, he's speaking literally. It is our *dharma*, our duty to ourselves and to the community, to open up to the point where we follow Christ's suggestion without even trying.

So that's where we can start our practice of coming together. I am you and you are me. We can't help but love each other, if only we would pay enough attention. That hard rain falling down on us all? It's here to wash the dust from our eyes and nourish our growth.

Now let's keep talking about how to get along.

3

We don't know

We have started out with an effort to, however imperfectly, write some words that wave in the direction of ultimate reality. No-self, God, truth, emptiness—we can call it what we like. Whatever words we use, though, hopefully there is something about them rings true.

But that only gets us so far. While many of us are still living in the realm of thinking and belief, even a pretty belief like universal oneness doesn't mean much of anything on its own. It's only an idea; as empty as the rest of our thoughts. To get to the truth, we need to expand beyond just thinking into feeling and being.

So having tried to point towards the mountaintop, even from a distance, we're now going to take things in what might feel like the opposite direction: not-knowing.

Most of us spend our lives making a fair effort at knowing. We learn how to read and write, how to tie a tie, how to miss a free throw. We like to think that we know ourselves: our story, our values, our hopes and dreams. We want to know right from wrong and how best to live.

Knowing can be vast. We can take knowing to the far edges of space with the science of cosmology or learn the workings of the smallest particles through the study of physics. We can know a half-dozen languages or how to cook a ten-course meal or how to change a flat tire in the rain with our eyes closed. We can relive the past in our minds and tell ourselves that everything could have been different, if only we had known, or dream of that perfect future that we know we will surely one day reach.

But how far does all of our knowing really take us? Not far enough. When they say there are no atheists in foxholes, that's not fair. Some might call the Buddha himself an atheist. Even God is just a belief that tries to get at the truth, not the truth itself. The Hebrew word for God, Yahweh, is traditionally not spoken or read aloud because hey, what's the point? When we try to put the divine into words, we can't help but fall short.

But no one facing a dark night of the soul is satisfied with knowing. There aren't enough facts or fantasies in the world to fill the void that gnaws at us from within. A restless mind fed a diet of information stays restless. The weasels knock at the door and we can only drown out the sound for so long. What good is knowing then?

So a first step to expanding beyond knowing is one we can take right now: saying, "I don't know." That right there, speaking those three words, "I don't know," is an act of liberation. However subtly, we're stepping beyond thinking, beyond reason, and beyond knowledge into, well, we don't know! What is beyond thought? We can call it being, or even Being, but what is being, really? We don't know!

We can go deeper and ask another question too: "Who am I? If we're honest, the answer to that is almost certainly, "I don't know. I don't know who I am." Sure, we have layers of identity,

13

but what is all that actually standing on? We don't know!

Asking ourselves, "Who am I?" is a fascinating opportunity for the kind of self-enquiry that Ramana Maharshi says can take us to the mountaintop. But it also helps us start to soften, even if just a little at first, and to move away from thinking of ourselves as actors in our own little dramas. All the world may be a stage, and we may be players, at least for now, but we don't have to take it so seriously.

This is where our relationship with each other and the community starts to come in. Most of us walk around carrying some sense of how things should be. That sense is usually in conflict with how things actually are, and that conflict creates a good deal of suffering in our minds.

But the suffering doesn't stop there. We bring it with us when we encounter those around us. We don't live in castles, after all. The line where you stop and I start is blurry for even the most materially-minded of us.

We can see this first in our families and close relationships. A disagreement among partners or siblings over whose turn it is to do the dishes can turn into a cold war. "I'm right and you're wrong," has a strength to it, but it's a brittle kind of strength and one that is prone to snap under pressure. I may think I know what's best, but if I want to co-exist with you, I'm going to need to learn to bend.

We see the same thing in our politics. There is an ebb and flow between periods of intense political division and those when things seem a little calmer. Today, as I write, it feels as though the intensity has been turned up to 11. Why? For so many of us, politics has become our way of interpreting the world and our place in it, a way we can define ourselves and our community. We do that by saying, "this is how things should be, and if our team wins, the world will be better for it." We may even start to think that passing (or repealing) the right laws is all that stands between us and the promised land. We can get so caught up in being right that we forget who we're busy trying to defeat: us.

What makes this all the more confusing is that politics does matter. All that word really means, after all, is the process of people coming together to make decisions about how to get along and organize the community that we are all a part of. We can't ignore politics because it's a part of living together. The decisions we make affect our lives: a school built here, a bus line routed there, a war started, a famine ended, justice served or denied. Politics touches all of us. All of us are citizens of the here and now.

That means that we need to look out for each other. Helping each other matters. The hungry must be fed. The homeless given homes, the sick treated, the lonely embraced. If we even begin to see the nature of self clearly, we can start to see the joke at the heart of politics: that those who urge us to love the other and those who tell us it's every man for himself are pointing towards the same thing. If we have an honest sense of no-self, we can be as selfish and self-centered as we want. Why? Because once we see that the other is us, we will know that looking out for number one means loving the other. Who is hungry? We are. Who is homeless? Us. Who is lonely? The God that doesn't see.

But when we get fixated on the how and the who of all of it, we start to suffer. When we become so certain that we must turn left, we torture ourselves when things go right instead. When we get too caught up in what we know and believe that we're all solid, then we end up blaming each other, getting angry with each other, hating each other even. All because the river turned the way it did.

So saying, "I don't know," not just about ourselves, but about society as a whole, is a way of softening to the community and the twists and turns of life. Martin Luther King speaks of the beloved community or what Christ calls the kingdom of heaven; what Malcolm X sees when he goes to Mecca: a place where we all get along. But none of us can claim to know exactly how the beloved community unfolds. We can say that it has to happen here, because where else? We can say that it has to happen now, because when else? But exactly what the road looks like, I don't know. Do you?

When we admit that, when we say, "I don't know," we inject humility and a sense of openness into the whole process. The ups and downs of politics and living in the community, which don't seem to be going away anytime soon, don't have to feel so heavy. That bend in the river we're afraid of? It will swing back around in time, and we just may see some ducks along the way.

We do what we can to help. We nurture and honor our intuition and where it leads us. We do our best to speak the truth and admit when we're wrong. We love as much as we can and as big as we can. But we do it all wrapped, gently, in "I don't know." As Krishna tells us, we act and renounce the fruits of action.

We do our best. We don't know what comes of it. We don't know. That's the adventure and the mystery. That—right here and now—opens us up to the new.

4

Don't take any of it too seriously

If we think of ourselves as part of a community at all, we probably give that community a specific definition. We might be residents of a neighborhood. Members of a church or mosque. Citizens of a country, a nation, or a tribe. Part of a culture. We think of ourselves as belonging to specific groups, in other words, and those group identities become part of how we define ourselves.

We also like to think of those groups as solid. America, for example, has been around for hundreds of years in one form or another. Indeed, many countries have. Some would date the present international order of nation-states that at least pretend to respect each other's boundaries to the Peace of Westphalia in 1648. That's a long time! Seems pretty sturdy, right?

Well, until we look at the longer arc of history and the rhythms of life. Then we start to remember that nothing is separate and everything changes. Much like our personal identities, our group identities (and the stability of the groups that we're identifying with) are revealed as hollow when we start paying attention and asking questions. Along with "Who am I?", we can ask, "What is my group?" or "What is my country?"

We can answer these questions with ideas, but there's nothing concrete to stand on there. We can't even agree on the same ideas. Ask any ten people what America is, and you'll likely get ten different answers and a whole range of feelings. Some say we're a shining city on a hill and others an engine of oppression. Who's right? Who's wrong? Depends on where we stand.

There's the story about the blind men and the elephant. Three blind men are examining an elephant. One feels the sharp tusks and calls the elephant dangerous. One wraps his arms around a leg and calls him strong and powerful. One feels his skinny little tail, laughs, and says, "What's the big deal?"

Our groups, our countries, our communities are like that. Look from one direction and we see good. Look from another and we see bad. From a third, well, who cares?

What does this add up to? Don't take our group identities so seriously. Don't take our personal identities so seriously either, for that matter. Identity is a product of where we're standing, and where we're standing changes from moment to moment.

This is what the Buddha is pointing towards when he talks about impermanence. Everything that has a beginning has an end. Nothing gold can stay. In other words, whatever group we're caught up in being a member of has a shape we can't agree on and isn't going to last. Not forever. Our community is always changing.

We might read this and think, "Well, then none of it matters." Why bother trying to be a decent member of the community (or one at all) if it's all going to disappear into the mists of time anyway? Fair enough. But today, here we are, here and now. We're probably not going to die today and even if we do, we don't have any way of knowing we won't end up right back here tomorrow.

So we've got to make the most of it, for our own sake, if for nothing else. Because who wants to be miserable? None of us, not really. Even if we live alone out in the desert, we still need a healthy community to support us: people to make the clothes we wear, grow the food we eat, and give us a hug when we need one. The Buddha tried cutting himself off from people and depriving himself of almost all human necessities in order to become enlightened. It didn't work. He lost fifty or sixty pounds but he wasn't free. It was only when he started saying yes to a daily gift of food brought by a woman living near his bodhi tree that he was able to achieve the awakening he sought. We can't be divine until we say yes to being human, too.

Here's another paradox: we matter and don't matter. Society matters and doesn't matter. It's all dust in the wind, but if we're hungry today, we still need a meal. There's no getting around that. We still need that hug too. We can't just not care because that won't fill our hungry bellies or warm our hearts. We also can't take everything so seriously that we're walking around crushed under the weight of our self-importance. Who can live like that? Many of us, for a while, I suppose, but at a certain point, we just get tired. I do, anyway. Don't you?

If we want to be honest and have an honest relationship with each other and our community, we must accept the impermanence and the openness of it all. That's the emptiness that the Buddha talks about. Not a meaningless void, but a friendly, playful, endless opportunity for change. A garden where creation and destruction come together to join at the core of who we are.

To really be free, too, we also have to meet that impermanence with love. Boundless, endless love, that pours out of us like a river. A love that says yes to whatever is: to everything that is here and now. As the Twelve Step tradition reminds us, "Acceptance is the answer to all of our problems." There is great power in loving what is. We might be scared to love that boldly, but if we're willing to take the risk, we will find that we have the power within us to back it up. All we have to do to start is take a breath and say, "Yes, this is what's happening now." Then, "And I meet the now with love."

We can't count on anything that has a form but we can count on love and acceptance. That, and laughter. We can take all of it with a large grain of laughter. There is so much we can get worked up about; much, even deservedly so. But it's all okay in the end. Really, it's all okay right now. When Taliban fighters blew up the 1500-year-old statues of the Buddha that were carved into a cliff in Afghanistan, most of us were horrified at the destruction. But the Buddha says, delightedly, "Yes!" Nothing lasts and that's deeply, totally okay.

Sacred cows are meant to be tipped. That keeps them from blocking the sun. How could anything hurt God, anyway? There is no authority, no Christ or Mohammed on the mountaintop: no one who is above us. There is no higher wisdom than what we all already hold within us. The Buddha is unemployed and sleeping outside when he wakes up to the truth within. Does that stand in his way? No. Does he have something we don't? No!

So we can laugh along with the Buddha when the statues fall. We can move through the world with a lightness that comes from being rapscallions or playful scoundrels as well as earnest servants. We can see the humor and the impermanence inherent in our society, our culture, and our institutions. That, right there, is itself an act of service. We need more laughter in the mix, because there is so much wisdom in laughter.

Shakespeare's fools are usually the characters that make the most sense. Are we bold enough to listen and follow their lead?

Better yet, can we come to see each other as rapscallions, as silly agents of God? Servants of Allah? Embodied emptiness? It doesn't matter. Do what we can, and enjoy the cosmic joke. We're in on it, whether we know it or not.

5

We're stuck

Since we're playing with paradoxes, let's take a look at another one: there is suffering and there is awakening (or liberation from suffering). We're all one, unified, perfect whole that holds space and time within and embodies infinite, eternal, unconditional love. We're also lonely, torn up, hungry, hurt, scared, disgusted, and angry. All at once, often.

We may think that these truths contradict each other. Surely suffering and the end of suffering are in conflict, right? If we give them both room to breathe, though, we can start to see that they come together in perfect harmony. One leads to the other. As much as we may hate the suffering, it is actually our invitation to wake up and be free.

We may have heard that we've got to acknowledge that we have a problem in order to do anything about it. That's good advice. If we want to be free, we have to start to say yes to suffering. We have to stop burying our heads in the sand (no disrespect to ostriches) and start paying attention to what is.

For many of us, turning to face our suffering, even hesitantly and squinting a little, is where our spiritual path begins in earnest. Indeed, the truth that we are suffering is the first of the Buddha's four Noble Truths that make up the heart of his teachings. Stop, take a breath, and see the suffering in our lives, he urges us. How else can we know that we need to look for a way out?

Likewise, the recovery community puts suffering in the first of the Twelve Steps, asking us to admit that we're powerless: over alcohol, drugs, sex, money, relationships, whatever it is that we're struggling with. The details of our struggle are less important than simply the fact that we're struggling and we're hurting because of it. We're not in control and we suffer when we try to pretend otherwise.

We don't have to approach suffering from any particular spiritual tradition though. We can just throw up our hands and say, "Hey, I'm stuck." Life is never exactly the way we want it to be, and try as we might, we can't ever fully bend the universe to our will. That can be really frustrating! But it's only frustrating because we keep trying to fight our way through. If we say, "I'm stuck," that, right there, is a moment of honesty and surrender that opens us up to something new.

When we talk about suffering, we're talking about a broad spectrum. Suffering can mean anything from living in a war zone to losing a best friend to not getting enough sleep or locking our keys in our car. Suffering can be the blues, the fear that gnaws at us in the night, the dragon we can't stop chasing, or just a quiet inability to be at ease with the present moment. Even more interesting (and subtle): suffering can come from going up as well as falling down. We might feel great when we get high or go on a good date or get a raise (or, say, write a book that talks about suffering). We've got something that's going to make things better now! But that buzz always goes away and

23

we're left wanting more, and if we get hung up on that, that, right there, is suffering.

If we're in a lot of pain, "I'm stuck" might not feel like enough. Then we can say something like, "This weight is just too much for me to carry," or "I can't hold it together anymore." We can even be bold and outright say to ourselves, "I am not enough." What isn't enough? The person we think we are. Our framework for how we operate in the world can't hold up any longer. Why? Because it is limiting us. Believing ourselves to be solid and permanent is a turn of the mind that doesn't serve us. That's okay. Let it go.

We suffer when we want things to be other than how they are. That brings us pain, maybe a lot, or maybe just a little. Either way, if we want that to change, we're going to need to stop trying to hide from the pain long enough to take a look at it.

That looking helps kickstart our spiritual journey, at least the deliberate, conscious part of it. Of course, as Adyashanti tells us, the funny thing is that we're looking for the truth about our suffering with God's own eyes. The spiritual journey is a circle, returning us to the place we began, only to see it in a new way.

Really, it's more a dot than a circle, since we're never anywhere but here and now. There is nowhere else to go. X marks the spot where we're already standing. We're all perfect Buddhas: if only we would pay attention!

Of course, most of us are not paying such close attention, and that's where the suffering comes in. On the most basic level, we suffer because we don't know who and what we are. We're confused and blinded to our own divinity and the infinite openness of our nature.

If there is such a thing as original sin, it is simply that confusion and blindness, which gives birth to all of the thousand forms of suffering we see in the world. That's it, right there. Suffering isn't about good and bad. We don't suffer because we're inherently mean or cruel or evil. We're mean or cruel or evil because we suffer.

Suffering is not a moral failing. We suffer because we don't see. We're in pain because we get so lost in who we think we are that we forget to just be. We think being isn't enough. The thing is, though, being is all that there is.

"Forgive them father, for they know not what they do," Christ cries out from the cross. They know not what they do. That's the whole truth of suffering. We hurt Christ because we don't understand that we're really hurting ourselves. We hurt ourselves because we don't know what we are. We think we get to pick and choose; to say yes to some of what is and no to the rest. But when we stop fighting with reality, as Christ does when he goes willingly to the cross, when we clear our eyes and open our hearts and feel the truth, our suffering blows away in the wind and we also stop doing each other harm. That is not the end of pain; we may still get sick or break our hearts. But it is the end of the pain we cause by flailing around blindly in the dark. That is no small matter.

So our task is to see clearly and feel what is true. It isn't a question of acquiring the right beliefs or learning the right lessons. The whole game is simpler than that. All we need to do is what Michelangelo did when he made David from a block of marble: carve away all the parts of the stone that weren't David. For us, that means saying yes and letting our suffering and our daily existence strip away all of our illusions until there's nothing left but what is. It sounds funny, but suffering helps lead us out of suffering.

Oddly enough, too, is that part of what we can allow to be

carved away is our beliefs about suffering, the nature of reality, our own divine perfection, all of it. Those beliefs can point us in the right direction and encourage us, but they can't carry us through the door. At a certain point, they just get in the way, because a belief—any belief, no matter how pretty—is just an idea. It can only gesture towards reality. It can't be real.

That's where our not-knowing comes to the rescue. Any belief we hold on to will eventually be shaken. Instead of being afraid when that happens, we get to say, "You know what? I don't know!" and let that belief, too, fall from our opening hands. We don't have to push away our beliefs, just not take them too seriously and allow the process to unfold.

As caring members of the community, too, we can't help but look around and see that there is suffering in our society. There is division and hurt. There are people not getting along, for silly reasons and for good ones. There are people who are hungry, scared, angry, afraid. There is pain and the hate that comes from it. There is loneliness.

The good news is that if we're willing to say "I'm stuck" as individuals, we're probably not going to be saying it alone. Our society is stuck too. All of us are touched by suffering. Maybe we're standing on the corner begging for a few dollars so we can eat. Maybe we're walking by feeling guilty. Maybe we're looking out our window worried about our property value. Three different parts of the elephant, sure. But it's all one elephant.

"I'm stuck" is really "We're stuck." We want to see this clearly because it is true and because it is the first step in liberating not just ourselves but our society, our earth, all of us. We're caught in this mess together. Acknowledging that may go against instinct: many of us try to ignore the suffering in our community. But does closing our eyes ever solve anything? Of course not.

Telling ourselves there is no suffering won't actually make the suffering go away, but it will get in the way of our awakening. So we need to look honestly at the state of things. We need to develop the presence of mind to take the moment as it is.

But balance matters. We don't want to drown in suffering either. That's easy enough to do, and it starts when we hold on to our suffering; when we make the suffering part of our identity and live in the story of our suffering. When we see the man (who's really us) begging for money and think to ourselves, "How sad," that's natural (until the day comes when we're the ones begging. Then we're thinking, "Help me!"). But when we turn that thought into a story and spend half an hour complaining to a friend about the whole situation, we're not helping anyone. We're just telling a story, rather than being with what is. If we help, help. If we walk on by, walk on by. If we beg, beg. We don't need to make a show out of it.

So we can be mindful about how we relate to suffering. This is a great opportunity to practice not taking things too seriously. We want to see suffering but we can learn to approach softly. That is part of our practice too: honoring the truth of suffering without getting (more) stuck in the suffering. Pain, discontent, fear, confusion—all of that is part of what is, yes, but it isn't the whole story.

At this point, we probably find ourselves asking what we do about suffering. Well, there are a lot of answers to that question, but a good place to start is by being open to what is. If, as our pretty beliefs tell us, the entire universe is really us, then the entire universe wants us to wake up and see that. What do any of us want more, after all, than to truly know ourselves? By being open to the truth and to the here and now, what we're doing is getting better acquainted with ourselves. We get to carry what we find with us into our community.

From one side of the elephant, everything happening in our lives and in our community is nothing less than a call to awaken. It's all happening, right here, right now, and all we have to do is say yes to all of it. Yes to the suffering. Yes to liberation. Yes to loving one another. Yes to taking that next breath.

6

We are the mud and the lotus

Thich Nhat Hanh reminds us that without the mud, there is no lotus. Without the dirt and the worms and the muck, the flower cannot grow. It's all one seamless, interconnected whole.

Likewise, the Buddha tells us in the Heart Sutra that there is no purity and no impurity. We can't be just one or the other because we hold both within us. Yeah, we want liberation. But we can't wake up without the suffering that serves as an alarm clock ringing in our ears. If we look with our Buddha-eyes, we see that there is never a this *or* that. There just *is*: one, continuous is-ness. A big night out at a fancy restaurant doesn't exist without some tired folks in the kitchen and a pile of garbage out back. We can't wall off any part of life from the whole.

If that sets our heads spinning, yes! But we don't have to crack the case, just take a look around. Have we ever succeeded in being fully pure (or impure, for that matter)? Has anyone we know? What exactly is the line between the two, anyway?

Ourselves, our communities—no piece of it is separate from the rest. In the Twelve Step tradition, there is a prayer that begins, "My creator, I am now ready for you to have all of me, the good and the bad." We can stop trying, in other words, to be a good person (or a bad person), because we don't need to be better than we are. We can't be. Despite our best efforts, we're never above anyone or any of it. There is no light without darkness. All any of us can do is aim to accept all of ourselves and to act from that place of wholeness. We can just be, whole. That's everything.

The same goes for the people around us we might not like. Sure, we can ignore them or try to stay away, and sometimes that's the right call. But none of us are really going anywhere and we all have a part to play in the great dance going on around us. There is no one among us who should not be here on this earth: good, bad, ugly, gross, or all of the above. How do we know this? We're all here and there is nowhere else to go! We can extend the prayer and say, "My creator, I am now ready for you to have all of us." What we're actually saying is that we're ready for *us* to have all of us.

Here's a fun practice we can try. As we look around at the suffering in our society, as we feel our own wounded hearts and see the same hurt in so many of our brothers and sisters, we can surprise ourselves and take a moment to say thank you: thank you for our suffering.

Even if we're on board with saying yes to suffering, this may seem a step too far. But hey, we're going for radical awakening here. If we want to be one with God, we should start acting like it. We've got to jump off the cliff at some point. Why not now?

So, let's try it by saying thank you for suffering. Begrudgingly at first, perhaps. Through gritted teeth, even. But the suffering is part of what is happening, here and now, and if we're going to be free, we've got to make peace with the present moment. When else is there? Where else is there?

Then, if we want to take a bigger leap, we can go even further. We can say thank you for the people who make us suffer. Now, when we say that people make us suffer, are we contradicting all the stuff in the last chapter about ignorance being the cause of suffering? A little, but not much. Ignorant people hurt each other, right? If you hit me, it won't sting any less if I understand it's really just the left hand punching the right. Our suffering comes from not seeing. But that suffering can take on many shapes, and many of those shapes involve us harming each other.

If we want to be loving members of the community, then it's a good idea to practice loving the community as a whole. That's where thanking the people who make us suffer comes in. It's easy to love the people who look out for us, but we're aiming bigger than that. Loving only the people who are on our side is still taking sides.

If we're taking sides, we're still not seeing clearly. We're not loving clearly. We all have needs, opinions, and preferences. That is a part of what is happening. But we don't ever need to take any of it personally or too seriously.

Why? We've got to see through our personalities and even our desires to really awaken. We have to understand that from a God's eye view, there are no sides. Just partners in a dance. So those people who have hurt us or who we stand against? We've got to see that they are within us and therefore loving them is not just a pretty ideal, but a practical necessity. We don't ever have to reject the whole. Truth demands that we don't.

If this feels like we're starting to go off the deep end, we are. But that's the thing: we need to go beyond reason and reasonable love into unreasonable love. Crazy love. Reason alone, as useful as it is, hasn't gotten us far enough. We need to

31

add the unreasonable, the crazy, the foolish even, into the mix. We need numbers and music and we need to find the song in the numbers and the numbers in the song and then throw it all out the window and laugh about how silly we can be.

We need to go deeper than reason, not just in our hearts but in our minds as well. What we're looking for is not intellect or cleverness but wisdom: true, deep, eternal. Wisdom and love, the mud and the lotus. Which is which? Depends on where we're standing.

"Wisdom," Jack Kornfeld tells us, "says we are nothing. Love says we are everything. Between these two, our life flows." Love demands of us a radical acceptance so great that we follow Christ's lead and love those who hurt us. Wisdom reminds us that none of it is personal anyway. No one is hurting us and no one is being hurt. There is hurting and there is hurt, and our task is to hold it all in our hearts so that we can be free.

We can play with the *tonglen* practice: breathing in the bad and breathing out the good. Breathe in the suffering, breathe out the liberation. Breathe in the hurt, breathe out the love.

****

There is a wonderful Buddhist story that I first read years ago in a book by Pema Chodron. A monk spends his days and nights meditating in a cave. One day, he wakes up to find that demons have moved into the cave with him. Flustered, he tries to go about his meditation but finds the demons too distracting.

So he sets out to teach them the dharma: the way things are. He shares all sorts of beautiful spiritual teachings with them. The demons just hoot and holler and get busy making dinner.

The monk gets frustrated, then angry. He shouts at the

demons and waves a stick at them, trying to drive them away. They just laugh louder. This goes on for a while.

Eventually, despairing, the monk sits down on the floor of his cave. "Fine," he says, "I give up." The demons suddenly go quiet. "I guess we're all just going to have to learn to get along," the monk says.

To his great surprise, the demons spread their wings and fly away. All except one. The biggest demon. The one who isn't so easily moved. But in that moment, the monk knows what to do. He walks over to the demon. They lock eyes for a moment, and the demon smirks. But then the monk steps into the demon's mouth. "Eat me," he says. "Go ahead."

The demon vanishes.

****

We are all the monk in the cave. Really, we're all the demons too, or at least the demons are part of all of us. We play both roles. When we say thank you for those that make us suffer, we're also saying thank you for that part of ourselves. This helps us to soften and allow ourselves to be whole. That is an act not just of forgiveness but of love.

We can never escape the demons, but we can be present with them. Feel them, sit with them, and invite them into our bodies and our hearts. There is nowhere else for them to go. Even the worst things are part of our divine wholeness. There is room for everything within each of us.

We don't want to forget to say thank you for those we love either, of course. Or for those we simply don't care much about. Or those we don't know. But we can take a leap towards radical, ridiculous love by offering thanks for those who hurt us, those who scare us, those who make us feel like we're not enough.

They are shaking our worlds, crying out to us to look towards the kingdom of heaven.

7

Action and acceptance

The last chapter ends with a big implied question hanging over our heads. Yeah, sure, radical acceptance and unconditional love sound nice. But we see people getting hurt in our community every day. We might be getting hurt! Are we just supposed to take it?

No. We're not. Yes. We are.

This is where we can really play with wisdom and love coming together. Wisdom, after all, begs us to take our hand from a hot stove. If it hurts, pull away. Simple.

Love, on the other hand, would have us love what is. Love the pain in the hand, even. Sure, it hurts, but it's what's happening. If we really want to have fun with it, we can also flip the formula around and say that love calls us to take our hand off the stove while wisdom demands that we practice acceptance. Silly, yes! There is laughter at the heart of everything.

What are we to make of this dance between action and acceptance? Well, that's a great question to consider. Part of an answer, at least, lies in what Krishna tells his friend Arjuna in the Bhagavad Gita. He urges him both to act and to renounce the fruits of action. We can take that as: show up, do our best, and don't worry about how it turns out. There is action that must be taken, but there is also never anything in it for us. We're not going to gain or lose any part of our Being and we don't get to determine the outcome. Action, too, is empty. Who is the actor? No one! Where can action take us? Nowhere but here!

My friend Norman loves to smile and say, "Let's see how it all plays itself out." The man devotes his life to serving others: helping people to recover from the hurt and pain of addiction with a hug and a kindly ear. He takes action. But he doesn't worry about the results. He knows that he isn't going to get anything out of it and that he is not in control of what happens. The fruits of his actions don't matter to him because he is at ease with himself and content to love those around him. What more could he possibly need?

So Krishna offers us good advice, if easier said than put into practice. But what does this have to do with harm and suffering? Well, of course, if we want to come from a wise, loving place, we do everything we can to not cause suffering. In our society, that means being mindful of our actions, not just as lip service, but with the understanding that what we do always affects those around us. That also means taking action to end suffering, both in our personal practices and in how we relate to the broader community. We pull our hands away from the burning stove without a second thought. We give the time of day to the woman living on the street (and a ten if we have it). We vote with an aim to help us all. If we see the truth, we share it.

But we also want to recognize that no matter what we do, there is still suffering in the world. The day may well come when the entire earth awakens to its own inherent unity, when the mountains and the fields sing and dance and the lion and the gazelle meet as friends, but it doesn't seem to be here yet. Not, at least, as of this writing. We're still hurting each other.

So there is a balance: taking action to end suffering without holding on to the expectation of being free from suffering. Why? Because we have to act to end suffering, but if we hold on to a particular outcome (even if that outcome is ending suffering), we create more suffering. If we pull the hand away from the hot stove and expect the pain to disappear right away, yes, we've acted, but we're going to be upset when the hurt lingers. We can walk the line between getting so far off in the spiritual clouds that we're putting up with nonsense and so lost in the daily struggle that we forget to breathe. Don't hold on and don't push away.

If this is all a little head-spinning, yes. The dance of action and acceptance—of surrender and doing what's right—is a great opportunity to practice our friendly principles of not knowing and not taking anything too seriously. Here, we get to recognize that we're doing our best and we're making mistakes and that it's all okay. If we step back far enough, the whole world is a spiritual playground for us to play on. Our right steps and our missteps are all part of the greater perfection.

If we don't see that right now, that's okay too. We get to say, I don't know! I don't know if any of this makes sense. I don't know if I'm right. I don't know if I'm wrong. I'm just going to show up for what's in front of me and let the chips fall where they may.

Sometimes, the chips can seem to fall skewed. Nelson Mandela showed up for the community and spent 27 years in prison as a result. Even he must have been surprised when he was set free and then sworn in as the president of South Africa a few years later. His example reminds us that the action is more

37

important than the outcome; that we can stand up for what is right and accept whatever happens as a result. He also shows us that change, that awakening, isn't neat or linear. A drop of water over here might burst a dam over there, but it follows a winding river to get there. We don't know how our actions will affect the world, but we can trust that they do.

Martin Luther King reminds us of this when he says, "I have been to the mountaintop. And I have seen the promised land. I may not get there with you. But I want you to know tonight, that we as a people will get to the promised land." He is telling us that we, too, can climb the mountain of awakening. We can serve, love, and accept whatever happens. We can do it together, as a community, one step at a time. We don't need to worry about how it all plays out because we'll get there in the end.

"And I'm happy tonight," Dr. King says. "I'm not worried about anything. I'm not fearing any man. Mine eyes have seen the glory of the coming of the Lord." He is shot and killed the next day. He knows this is coming; he must. He stands up anyway because he has surrendered himself to serving love and truth. What choice does he have?

Like the monk in the cave, Dr. King is willing to offer up his life to end suffering. He's free because he has seen through his fear and knows that there isn't anything to be afraid of. He isn't going to gain or lose anything; he's just doing the right thing because that's what a truly free person does.

We might be tempted to put people like Nelson Mandela and Dr. King up on a pedestal. But the power of their example is that they are just as ordinary as any of us. We too can cultivate that same willingness and freedom of spirit because the love that drove them lives in us.

Fortunately, perhaps, our sacrifices may not have to be so

dramatic. We don't all have to die violently in order to be free (although we're all serving time in prison until that freedom comes). We do have to be willing to take the right action and to accept what is, even if only a little bit at a time. Our dying can be gentle.

That last bit may be our saving grace (mine, anyway). We get to ease into this stuff. We get to take it slow, because the suffering isn't going to go away until we're all the way done. The game just keeps going until the last demon has vanished, and that means we get to play at our own pace. If we're ready to organize our community or march for peace and justice, great. If not, great. We can work at a food bank or at a hedge fund. Either way, the universe will keep feeding us opportunities to act and accept, to practice love and wisdom, to offer ourselves up to the whole.

If the demons come, we say thank you. If they don't, we say thank you.

8

Taking a good look at ourselves

If we've come this far, we've at least started to open up to our own inner sense of universal oneness, of no-self. We also have some awareness of suffering, both ours and our communities. We are starting to see that our suffering is a question of ignorance or blindness, not of innate ill character. What now?

This is a good opportunity to start really taking an honest look at ourselves: to pay attention. We can call this mindfulness, self-enquiry, being present, looking inwards, whatever we want. The point is that we want to start observing ourselves. Rather than just being the actor, going about our business, we can start cultivating our inner witness.

Ramana Maharshi teaches that achieving spiritual awakening can be as simple as continuously putting our attention on our inner sense of "I" or "I am", and asking, "Who am I?" Ram Dass tells us to be here now, like Eckhart Tolle, who urges us to simply be present. All of them are pointing to the here and now because that's where the truth lies. That's where God and our joining with God lies. We want to be with what is because that's how we start to not just believe in oneness and unity, but to feel it.

In other words, it's a good idea to start directing our attention inside ourselves, not just as a meditation practice but throughout our day. We can practice watching our thoughts, feeling our feelings, being in our bodies, being with all that is inside us. This helps us feel more grounded and be more aware of how we're conducting ourselves with those around us.

Here's a fun practice: Twelve Step groups teach an exercise called an inventory. When we do an inventory, we write down all of our resentments: all the people we don't like and everything we don't like about them. We write down how all that affected us. Then, and here's the good part, we write down our part. What we had to do with all of it. The harm we've caused. When we're done, we share it all with someone we trust and have a good laugh.

This is an interesting exercise because it encourages us to take a more holistic look at ourselves and where we are. It's a good way to cut through thinking of ourselves as existing in a narrative, usually where others are to blame, and to practice observing ourselves more honestly. It's also a great way to start to loosen up about ourselves and to recognize that we don't have to fit some inhuman ideal of perfection. We've screwed up plenty and that's okay.

We do this exercise so we can start integrating a more open, honest perspective into our daily lives. Asking ourselves, "What's my part?" in a conflict is especially helpful when it comes to living in the community. After all, most of us like to think of ourselves as the hero of our life story. But if we're the heroes, that means somebody else has to be the villain. If we're all thinking that way, that leads to conflict, quickly.

So when we ask, "What's my part in this?", we're putting ourselves on equal footing with one another. We're cutting through the hero and villain narrative, and recognizing that we're not above any trouble that's gone on. We might have even started it. This, too, points us towards oneness: we're not separate from anything, even the stuff we'd rather not admit to.

A key part of any process of looking at ourselves is making the effort to be honest with ourselves. This just means that we have to learn to be honest about everything, even the parts of our experience that we would rather ignore or run away from. It can be very helpful to have someone in our lives that we trust enough to be completely open with, as this person can help us practice being honest. Ultimately, though, the person we really have to be totally honest with is us.

Of course, most of us aren't honest all the time because we're scared to be. What will happen, right? That's okay! We can nurture our honesty practice over time. It's just that, a practice. We'll get the hang of it more the longer we do it. We don't have to be the hare, just the tortoise. Easing in still gets us there in the end. If we feel that we must lie about something, we should remember the Buddha's advice to always be honest with ourselves about the fact that we're lying.

It's also important to remember that the truths we may be scared of are what we can call relative truths or little truths. A relative truth is something that may be true today, but won't be so forever. Let's say we're parking our car and we scratch the car next to us. Embarrassing? Yes. Scary, even, especially if we don't have insurance. But soon enough, the whole thing will fade into memory, and then the day will come when no one even cares that it happened at all.

"What's the weather out today," someone might ask. "Rainy,"

42

we say. "What was it yesterday?" "Sunny." What was true then is no longer true now. What, then, is there to be afraid of?

This will hold whether the truth we're running from is heavy or silly. Indeed, the fastest way to let a relative truth pass away is to acknowledge it and say, yes, this happened. Yes, this is true. Saying yes to an uncomfortable truth doesn't trap us in that truth; it sets us free and allows that truth to move along on down the road. This is because all of the relative truths of everyday life are just pointing towards the eternal truth that everything changes and nothing lasts. Saying yes to our relative truths helps us to see that and soften to the awareness that everything is truly, deeply okay.

What if we don't know the truth? Even better! We get another chance to practice not knowing and to allow ourselves to be open to uncertainty and, well, openness.

We can approach our practices of mindfulness, self-enquiry, and honesty from a lot of different directions. But one way or another, if we want to be free, we've got to turn our gaze upon ourselves. That's where the truth lies, inside us. Those villains we look down on, those other people we can't stand? Whatever we don't like about them is also in us. That's why we can't stand them! They are reminding us of our own multitudes, and our multitudes are not always pretty. We don't get to pick and choose; we either have to accept the whole of our being or fight with the reality of what is, and that's a fight we're never going to win.

We are the mud and the lotus, and that's okay. All the good and all the bad in the world exist within us. In our emptiness, our oneness, we hold good and bad and are beyond it, beyond all duality. The more we can see that there's room for all of it—that there is unity within the conflict—the more we're free.

The more we soften to all parts of ourselves, the more we see that none of it is the real us.

****

Speaking of something we'd rather not admit to: the more we start taking an honest look at ourselves, the more we will likely start to notice something uncomfortable. We're hypocrites!

We say one thing and do another. We believe all the right things, most of the time. We're kind, except when we're not. We're full of righteousness, and then fail to live up to our own standards. We might even write a book full of pretty words about spiritual principles and practices that can help us get along better and then fall (embarrassingly) short of embodying those words.

We may try to fight through our hypocrisy, or ignore it, or just hope it goes away. Maybe we even deny it completely or blame those around us. But once we develop a certain level of awareness, we're not going to be able to run. We know what's going on.

Where does our hypocrisy come from? The source of our suffering: the belief that we have a solid, separate self. That's the self that tells us, sure, let's go ahead and take a little more than I need. I deserve it, right? I know it's wrong, but it's only for me. No big deal.

But our community runs into trouble because all of us are thinking this way. If everyone takes too much, then there's not enough to go around. If we all operate like we're special, like we're above everyone else, we're going to start banging into each other really fast.

What do we do about our hypocrisy? A good place to start is

noticing it, and then having a good laugh. Better yet, share it with each other for some bigger laughs. Sure, we can try to force ourselves to be perfect, but that's probably not going to go very well. We're not hypocrites because we're morally flawed; we're hypocrites because we don't see clearly. We forget that there is room for all of us.

Really, our hypocrisy is a great barometer for our spiritual awakening. As long as we think we're exempt from the whole, we're going to keep being hypocrites. When it comes up, hey, that just means we're not quite there yet.

If we can be honest about where we are, excellent. That's a good practice and a big step forward in our circular journey home. We can't be here and now if we're pretending to be there and then.

We can get even more out of looking at our hypocrisy though. Our inconsistencies are also pointing directly to the truth of no-self. We go from being one person to another to another because we're not anyone in particular. We can't stay standing in one place no matter how hard we try. It's not possible. If we can see that, even better.

9

Being no one

We're not anyone in particular, huh? We've touched on this already, but come on: what if we want to be somebody? Isn't that the whole point of the game: to make something of ourselves and leave our mark on the world? To show the community who we are? To separate ourselves from the pack?

Well, sure. Yes. Right up until the moment we realize we can't. We're like Percy Shelly's Ozymandias (or Vince Gilligan's, for that matter): no matter how many monuments we build, the desert will swallow them (and us) in the end.

If we take an honest look at our own experience, we can start to see that we can never quite count on anything to define us. No achievement or part of ourselves is ever the real us. Hopefully, we can start to see that that's okay—that really, all we ever need to be is what the present moment brings out in us.

If we take an honest look at our fears, most of us will find that we are terrified of being not enough or being nobody. Being a nobody. So we spend our days trying to be someone, anyone, someone we can point to and say, yes, I exist. I matter. What are we more scared of: dying or being forgotten? The answer might well be a tossup.

But at the moment of death, if not before, we will find that all of our accomplishments, all of our memories, all of everything we think makes us someone, can't buy us another breath, another heartbeat. We've been no one the whole time, a nobody pretending to be a somebody because we don't realize that we don't have to be somebody. We can say yes to being nobody.

We don't have to wait for death to start saying yes to being nobody, of course. We're fighting our inherent nobodiness every day. What if we just stopped?

What does this mean? Well, think about all the time we spend every day trying to prop up our sense of who we are. We might work really hard at the gym because we're trying to achieve a particular image of ourselves. We might spend extra hours in the office because we want a promotion so we can earn the respect of our peers. We might end a relationship because we want a partner who makes us look better.

It's not that any of these actions are bad on their own. They're all just actions; energy at work. But when we act with attachment to a specific outcome or because we want a reward—when we get attached to the fruits of action—we lose sight of the truth. We think that we're somebody, going about our business and accruing points along the way, rather than just being part of the natural unfolding of the universe. We make it about us. We make it personal.

It's not personal. It's never personal because there's no one here. So many of us try so hard to be better than each other, but if we think that we're better (or worse) than anyone, we're lying. Why? Because we're all nobody. "No increasing, no decreasing," the Heart Sutra reads. We don't have anything to gain or lose. How can nobody gain? How can nobody lose? We're all one

47

anyway: is the left arm better than the right? Sure, we get stuck in thinking that we're somebody, but deep down, we know. We know we're not. As somebody, we'll never be enough. As nobody, we are perfect and complete.

We can say yes to that. Yes to knowing that we're nobody. Is that knowing or not-knowing? Who knows? When we do, though, the whole universe opens up, because the universe isn't anybody either. We're unified in our nobodiness. We're all empty.

That means being nobody is a friendly thing to do. If we're not stuck on being somebody, we're better able to serve and help the community. We're like a great bench player: just plug us in wherever and however we can help out.

So much of the conflict between us is because we're all trying to be somebody. When we feel our identities shaken, when no-self pokes us and we touch our own emptiness, we tend to blame each other because we think that something is wrong. We might even lash out or cause harm. No! We're not no one because of something someone else did. We're not no one because of anything. No-self is just the way things are. Feeling unsettled in our identities just means that we're seeing the truth.

For example, how much hurt do so many of us cause by trying to push away the feminine—inside and out—because we are afraid that our masculinity is empty? How much damage done: to ourselves, to our families, and to our community? Well, guess what? Masculinity (and femininity) is empty! It's not even ours. We are fighting to prop up a ghost that doesn't belong to us and creating a lot of pain while doing it. There is no masculine, no feminine, no duality. We can't isolate any aspect of the whole. We don't get to pick and choose. No division is real.

We're not solid, remember? There is no such thing as a secure, definitive sense of self. As long as we're trying to be somebody, we'll never be able to breathe easy. As nobody, though, well, we've got the power of the whole universe running through us. What do we have to worry about then?

The whole structure of our community softens when we start being nobody. We don't have to worry about status or position. At least not nearly so much, anyway. There's an old joke: what is the highest rank in a Twelve Step group? Member! Just show up and help out. Who cares about the rest? It isn't serving us anyway. It's just blocking us from our true, glorious nobody-nature.

10

What can we do to help?

So, let's say we're going to give being nobody a shot. How do we go about it?

Well, that may be the work of a lifetime, if not several. But one thing we can do is to soften: to stop resisting ourselves and running from that nagging sense that underneath our somebodiness, maybe we're not anyone after all. It's not that we don't still have a personality or preferences or any of that. But if we touch our inner sense of being nobody, even a little, we can start to know that we don't have to take our personality and our personal gains too seriously anymore. We don't have to disrespect that level of things, but it doesn't have to be our driving force either.

So we can soften our whole sense of being. We can say yes to being with what is and allow ourselves to be a part of what's happening in the present. We still have our memories, even some sense of somebodiness, but we wear that loosely, knowing it won't last any more than a pair of jeans will.

We can also soften to the community around us. We don't have to see each other as people we have to impress or sell some version of ourselves to. As we soften, we relate to each other not as a transaction, not as giving or receiving, but as part of the collective dance. When no one dances with no one, it's always perfect.

As a nobody, we can cultivate a servant's heart. We all have to serve one way or another, as Bob Dylan reminds us. What's better to serve than the community? A servant's heart is open to the possibilities inherent in each moment. It asks, "What can I do to help?"

That's a wonderful question, not only because it engages our hearts, but because it points us towards the truth that all of us, somebody or nobody, always has something to offer. If we're here, we're a part of it all, and if we're a part of it all, there's a role for us to play.

In other words, there's room for all of us in the community. More than that, we're all necessary. We each complete the greater whole, and we do that by embracing being nobody.

Being nobody isn't passive. Is a servant passive? Of course not. A servant is in the thick of it, one way or another. Our role in the community may look different depending on our circumstances. Some of us may have a few people in our lives; others may have dozens or hundreds. But whatever our community looks like at the moment, we can show up for it as nobody. We can show up with nothing much beyond a loving heart and ask, "How can I help?"

This doesn't mean throwing knowledge or expertise out the window. Knowing is useful. We need to know how to build homes, to grow food, to keep the trains running. But we can ground our knowing in not knowing. We can rest being an expert or a professional, being a someone, within our greater awareness of being no one. We can play our role and remember

51

that it's just a role.

If we're nobody, we don't have to take any of it too seriously. That leaves us with more room to love and to help. The stakes are lower; we don't care about looking a certain way anymore, so what else are we going to do?

So, how can we help?

11

Come on in

One way we can help (and practice being nobody, for that matter) is by learning how to say, "I was wrong."

This is another Twelve Step practice that can be very useful. Odds are, we've hurt those around us at some point or another. One thing we can do to clean things up: go to them and say, "I was wrong for doing that. I hurt you. What can I do to make it right?"

Making this kind of statement, as my friend Pamela reminds us, is different from simply saying sorry and trying to move along. The goal here is to sincerely acknowledge the harm that we've done and ask what we can do to correct it.

It is important to remind ourselves at this point that we don't cause harm because we're bad. Beating ourselves up is a waste of our time (and everyone else's). As the saying goes, "Get off the cross, we need the wood!" Sometimes, we hurt others by mistake or as the result of circumstance, but when we do so intentionally, it is because we have forgotten that we are one with whoever we harmed and that everything is okay in the land of here and now. If we always remembered that, we would never deliberately harm anyone! Our vision is what can go wrong. Trouble comes when we act while driven by fear, anger, confusion, or ignorance.

The Buddha teaches what he calls right view, which is part of the Noble Eightfold Path that can guide us in our awakening to the truth. Right view means seeing that we're all connected and our actions affect each other (and therefore, us). When we harm someone, then, it's because we've acted from what we could call wrong view. That's the original wrong: not something permanent in any of us but a temporary (if sometimes very long-lasting) state of blindness. When we do something wrong, we're not bad but inaccurate: wrong in the sense of a stopped clock or a missed question on a test, not an innate character flaw.

What if more of us were willing to admit when we're wrong? It's a vulnerable thing to do, for sure, because we're giving up trying to control what happens next and instead surrendering to the truth. But it's also a powerful action to take, because we're allowing the power of the truth to carry us. While we might be afraid of looking bad or weak, what we're actually doing is standing up and taking responsibility for the community. How wonderful to have the opportunity to do that, right? What a great example to set! The fact is, too, that admitting when we're wrong gives us the space to move forward and put the trouble behind us.

This practice is also a great way to get to know our inner nobody because it allows us to soften our own sense of righteousness: of having a solid self that's always in the right. When we say "I was wrong," "I hurt you," and "How can I make it right?", we're letting the air out of our own sense of inviolability and allowing ourselves to be ordinary. We all screw up or lose sight of what's right sometimes because that's just part of how

it is. But when we do, we don't have to run away: we can put up
our hand and say yes to being accountable, to being permeable,
to being part of the greater whole. By admitting it when we've
done wrong, we are able to fully join the community and also
give those around us permission to do the same.

Often, there is blame to go around. We've done wrong, yes,
but we've been wronged too. Our instinct might be to wait for
another to make the first amends, but that might be a long
wait. If we're going to break the stalemate, someone has to
step up. Why not lead the way? We can't force anyone else to
take responsibility, but we can show each other how it's done.
If our gesture is not returned, that's okay. We've taken action
and renounced the fruits of that action. Krishna is cheering us
on, and the rest is out of our hands.

Sometimes, though, what's needed is less a matter of weigh-
ing out right or wrong and more of simply listening. After
Nelson Mandela took office, the new South African government
established a truth and reconciliation commission in order to
give the country and the world the opportunity to bear witness
to all the harm that had gone on under the old apartheid regime.
This approach is part of a broader tradition of what is sometimes
called restorative justice that aims not to punish but to heal—by
honoring those who are suffering and honestly airing things
out so that everyone can begin to move forward anew. The goal
is to listen, not to judge, and to transmute pain into freedom
through the simple act of human awareness and compassion.
The truth really does set us free.

Bring the dark into the light. There is room for all of it and
all of us. When we see the man sitting outside the Twelve Step
meeting dressed in clothes that haven't been washed in weeks
and talking to himself, we might be tempted to recoil. No! We

can follow Pamela's lead and say, "Come on in!"

We can take that "come on in" spirit with us every day. Just as we offer our demons a home within us, we can practice taking in the suffering of the world. Doing so can be as simple as developing a willingness to listen to the pain of our fellows, not as judges but as nobody. All we need offer is a friendly ear and a wide-open heart with no agenda other than, "I hear you, sister. I hear you, brother."

This is especially important because we can't fix or change each other. We don't have that power: each of us is wherever we are at any given moment. But we can give each other the space to heal and the loving presence to nudge us along on our way.

When we listen to another talk about their suffering, we might not like what we hear. So what? We're giving that person room to breathe. What a gift! Yeah, they might say something silly, but who cares? Like we've never done that? Besides, if someone is in pain, do they need to be told they're wrong or given a hug? What would we want?

Just doing that, listening, holding that space, opens us up to the sacred silence and the eternal newness that is beneath all of our words and all of our pain. It's a practice, of course. We're probably not going to be great listeners all the time. Sometimes we get too caught up in what we're hearing or distracted by our own thoughts and tune out. But the practice of listening is a way to be present, to be here now, and to connect with God and each other.

Listening, after all, is giving the gift of silence, and silence is more powerful than words. Truth, ultimate truth, can't be spoken or written down. It is found only in silence; it is silence, because silence enfolds sound. Silence and emptiness hold all that there is within them. Silence is for all of us to share.

12

Unity through diversity

We may inter-be with each other, but from one side of the elephant, at least, we also seem very different. Indeed, many of us struggle with being a part of our community because we may see some among us as too different. Some of us, for example, may be afraid that the community is changing too fast, that there are too many new ideas or new members. Slow down! Others may think that some people in the community are too old-fashioned. Get with the times, right?

What we're all struggling with is the fact that the community itself isn't solid. We want it to be the way it was or the way we dream it could be. Instead, the community, like us, is here and now, always changing, shifting, escaping definition. We can't pin the community down any more than we can pin down ourselves.

But we can be grateful for the change, for all of our differences, for the thousand forms of God we see before us as we walk the streets of a crowded city or stand in the slow quiet of an empty field. All of it is coming together perfectly in this moment and asking us to see. Our outer differences reflect our inner diversity because the world is a mirror. Everyone we meet is showing us something about us. If we don't accept each other, then we're rejecting parts of ourselves. Without the churn, without the people who make us uncomfortable, we would be poorer.

There is a wonderful truth about trees. Plant a group of seeds from the same species of tree in neat little rows and they'll grow okay. But scatter seeds from a bunch of different species? They will grow faster and stronger and become a beautiful forest. The mess doesn't hold the trees back. It's what leads them to thrive.

We're no different. Sure, we'd like to be at ease all the time. But until we're truly free and content to be no one, that's not really an option. Every person who doesn't fit into our sense of how things ought to be is saying, "Wake up, wake up! You're still dreaming that you're someone. You're still not present. You still haven't surrendered to what is."

They are here to remind us that we are not in control: not of them, not of ourselves, and not of the community as a whole. We've touched on this idea once or twice already, but let's sit with it for a bit now: we are not in control of any of it. Yes! We might spend our whole lives trying to fix this, but the truth is, not being in control isn't a problem. We don't have to gain control and we couldn't if we tried.

Naturally, though, most of us don't want to hear that we're not in control. To that, I would simply ask: can you stop the sun from rising, keep yourself from aging, or make another change their mind against their will? Do any of us get to decide the outcome of action? Of course not. We just take our best shot and hope the ball goes through the net.

Again, this isn't a problem to be solved or fixed. We're stuck, right? We can't fight reality and expect to win. But there is another option. It may go against our instincts, but we can just give up trying to push the boulder up the hill and accept that we're not running the show. No one is! That's what the community is reminding us: all those people we dislike or even despise are literally God shouting at us that it is okay to bow to the flow of life and to accept the whole of the present moment. How kind of them!

So often we are afraid of each other because we remind each other that we're not in control; that we are inherently vulnerable. The solution, then, is to accept that lack of control. We're not enough, remember? Yes! That's what surrender really means. To lay down our arms and stop trying to beat ourselves and each other into whatever shape we believe is necessary.

Instead, we can practice looking around at the people in our community and thinking: "I don't have to try to control any of them. I don't have to try and make them be a certain way. I don't have to force myself to be a certain way. It's not up to me." Talk about a weight off our shoulders. What a relief!

Here's another way to put all of this: most of us think of our minds as being in command of our bodies. But if we wake up with an aching back, we get to see that we're actually at the mercy of the whole. We're not in charge of the body; if we were, the pain would be gone. Nothing is above the rest. There is no one sitting at the head of the table. The mind and the body are interdependent; there is no point where one starts and the other stops. Our bodies are always here to remind us of the truth.

The same is true for our community. None of us are in charge and we all depend on each other. Hey, we might be a big shot, but when we wake up one day and find that our pipes are clogged and sewage is flooding into our home, the plumber we might normally look down on becomes a savior. Do we know who grows the food we eat? Probably not, but we are alive because of their efforts. Not only is the emperor naked, but he isn't even the emperor. We all inter-are.

When we surrender our dream of being in control, we can give it up to Allah or God or Krishna if we want. But even that may still leave us hung up on the idea that someone, somewhere is in control. No! There is no subject and object: it's all empty! So we can make it even simpler than that and just surrender to what is: to the present moment that holds us all and is us. We're just saying yes to riding the wave instead of being knocked down by it. The present moment isn't about control; it's about being. For all of us, being is enough.

Indeed, here's a fun paradox: we don't have a solid self, but nothing in the universe matters more than our being. Not our being anything specific, or in any particular form, just being fully, completely present. The butterfly matters as much as the lion, the beggar as much as the king. Your being. My being. Not even yours and mine really, it's all just Being. Being, alone. There is no control because there is no one else to control Being and no one that isn't Being for Being to control.

Being is not up to me. It's not up to you. It's not up to any of us. It just is. All we can do is meet what is with love.

If we can start to take this perspective, then we can begin to have a new basis for getting along. Rather than getting worked up about the specific shape of the community, we can focus on the reality that we're all actually playing the spiritual game together. Our goal isn't to pave the streets with gold, it's to help each other wake up. When we think of it like that, we can start to see how that neighbor who rubs us the wrong way is actually a first-round draft pick for our team.

Many of us feel a particular frustration with people who see things differently than we do. But hey, we see what we see because of where we are standing. What a wonderful thing! We get to offer each other the gift of the view from different sides of the elephant.

Yeah, if we're on the outside looking in, we may not really want to hear what the comfortable have to say. If we're on the inside looking out, we might want to forget about those who are still out in the cold. But what a great opportunity to practice listening! When we're on the outside, we can help offer the truth of suffering. When we're on the inside, we can help remind each other that suffering isn't all that there is. Or we can flip it and see the suffering in our comfort and the liberation in living on the fringe. As crazy as our differing perspectives may make us, we can all help each other to get a clearer sense of the whole picture.

We can even start to seek out the people and situations that make us uncomfortable, because it's all just practice, right? Rather than avoiding the fire, we move towards it. We want to wake up, we want to see. The people who make us uncomfortable can help open our eyes.

To get anywhere with this practice, though, we have to be willing to let go. This is an opportunity to see how stuck we still are in being somebody. We've got an identity, not just as an individual but as a member of a group, a culture, with a past and a story and all of it. More than that, those around us are reinforcing that identity. Feeling all of that shaken up isn't just uncomfortable, it's painful.

We don't need to feel bad about that. Change is painful and scary; all the more so when we feel like the community we count on to sustain us is what's changing. We can honor the feelings that change brings up within us. When we see others struggling with those feelings, we can honor that too. Patience—with ourselves and each other—is key. We're all doing the best we can.

But if we're aiming for liberation (or even just for a community that gets along), we have to be willing to let go. None of us can stand on any of it. We have to be willing to soften and see the nobody inside even our most cherished identities. We don't have to push any of it away or pretend it isn't there, just know that we contain multitudes and exist beyond all categories and definitions. We are all our own opposites. That's the beauty of being nobody. That is freedom.

Living in a community with lots of different people and lots of different perspectives can also offer us a great chance to practice saying, "I was wrong," or "How can I help?" Doing so helps soften our rigid sense of who we are and how things should be, making us vulnerable to our inner nobodiness and shaking us out of our defenses. Each time we do this, we lower our castle drawbridge a little more.

Really, there is no castle, no drawbridge, no moat. We don't have anything to stand on or walk across. We do have deep wisdom and a heart full of love. That's all we need. The rest, all of it, can go.

13

A brief meditation

An interesting exercise we can do is to take a look at a map of the world. We'll see all sorts of lines: borders dividing metro regions, states, countries, all making up neat little units of organization. Everything is defined.

Then the rub: take a look at a satellite photograph of the same thing. All those borders are gone.

All of them, like all the divisions in our world, are man-made. Boundaries don't exist outside of our collective imagination. That doesn't mean that we don't deal with them on a daily basis, or that there is no point in having any sort of structure to the community, but it is a blaring message: don't take any of it too seriously.

From a God's eye view, none of it is real.

What we can see from satellite photos is the planet itself, and, if we zoom in enough, the forests and rivers and trees and fields and animals and towns and cities and people. There are no neat lines here, just a messy web of pulsating, vibrant life and death all blending together. Try as we might, we can't ever fully organize it or contain it or categorize it. Not really, because it's more than can be put into words or ideas. The best we can do is be with it. Love and serve. That's enough. That's all we've ever needed to do.

14

Every meeting is sacred

We've come a long way in a book that uses the word community a lot without saying much about the outlines of a strong
community. Everything we've talked about so far is aimed at
helping us open up to the truth about who and what we are so
that we're better able to love and get along with one another.
But what does that loving community look like in practice?

That's a big question. We can say, "I don't know," and there's
something to that. Who among us can claim to be a member of
an ideal community? None of us, right?

But just leaving it at "I don't know" is a bit of a cop-out. Our
community doesn't have to be perfect to be worth our time. Or,
rather, maybe we should consider that perfection doesn't always
look the way we think it does.

The Buddha teaches that we should look for guidance from
what he calls the three gems: the Buddha, the dharma, and the
sangha. The Buddha, of course, is our perfect, empty, awakened
nature, our universal oneness. The dharma is the teachings that
point us in that direction, the path we take on our journey of
awakening, and our duties along the way. The sangha is the

people we walk the road with.

So we can think of our community as a sangha: our companions in spiritual growth. Our sangha can take on many forms. If we're at the point where we're feeling a desire to awaken, even if only a little, then we would do well to have other people in our lives who are also spiritually curious. That's the most common sense of the word sangha or what the Twelve Step community calls trudging buddies: fellow travelers on the spiritual path.

That kind of community can be loose and informal, like a meditation circle or a recovery group or just a close spiritual friendship or two. It can also be more structured, like joining a monastery or religious community or going on meditation retreats. There's a lot of ways to do it and it's not a question of right or wrong, just of what encourages us in our practice and gives us a chance to contribute and open up.

But we can also widen the circle of what we consider our sangha. After all, some of us might think of ourselves as working towards enlightenment and liberation, and others might never give such notions the time of day. But we're all in this together, right? We're all drops in the ocean of God and we all hold the ocean inside ourselves. Whether we know it or not, whether we care or not, we're all on that road to nowhere that leads us to nirvana, shining within us right here and right now. Since enlightenment is simply finding out the truth about ourselves, how could it be any other way?

This means that really, the whole world is our sangha. Everyone is our community. Every action, every encounter, every relationship, whether for a moment or a lifetime, is an opportunity to practice, to see the truth. It's all here to help us wake up. In that sense, the whole universe is for us.

That's a lovely sentiment. But what can we do with that? Well, we can start living our lives that way. We can go about our days as we always have, but now we can approach every encounter as a spiritual experience. We can greet each other with our attention on the present moment and the person in front of us. We can hold the intention of "how can I help?", of listening, of giving space. We can soften to everyone we come across because whatever we think of each other, we're all trudging buddies.

To take it back to where we started, everyone we come across is us. Treat others as we would like to be treated, Christ tells us. How would we like to be treated? If we're honest, we know. We want to be loved unconditionally, accepted completely, and seen clearly. It doesn't matter who we are or what we think we might be. We all want to be loved.

So that's what we give to the community, to our sangha. We give love, we give not knowing and being nobody, we give a desire to help. We accept each other and what is and act from that place. But we do this without holding on to a result, because that's missing the point. Really, we remember that we're not giving and not receiving at all, just keeping the dance going.

If this sounds like a lot, yes. It is. But we don't have to do it perfectly. We get to do it imperfectly, terribly even. We just keep at it. Because we've got a sangha, we don't have to do it alone. We give to the community and the community in turn is there to sustain us.

In the Buddhist tradition, a bodhisattva is an awakening being who insists on being born again and again into a mortal life until all beings across the universe have become free. This sort of being chooses to plunge back into the suffering of ordinary life in order to help others escape from suffering. Talk about a big commitment! Unreasonable love, for sure. Crazy love, even.

What a bodhisattva understands, though, is that if all beings are one, none of us are really free until all of us are. Not completely free anyway. We don't have to live in an idyllic world in order to awaken ourselves. We don't have to be perfect or clean or pure. We can't be. We get to work with the mud and the lotus; to be both and more than both. But we do have to remember the sangha and work not just for our own liberation but the freedom of the whole community.

There is a fun meditation practice. Before we start meditating, we offer our meditation up as a sacrifice for the liberation of all beings. We close our meditation with that same offering. What are we sacrificing? Our small self: our delusions, our attachments, our beliefs, our sense of separation; who we think we are, in other words. We're offering it up as a sacrifice to our big Self: emptiness, God, unity; or what we really are. Why? Any sort of effort to practice mindfulness or pay attention to the present moment will slowly strip away our attachment to our small self. We might as well get on board with it and offer it up willingly. We are always at the mercy of the present moment. Yes!

Remember, God demands that Abraham sacrifice that which is most precious to him: his son Isaac. Of course, the joke is that God doesn't want to harm Isaac. He just wants Abraham to let go. Abraham's willingness and surrender is the point. When God sees that, he reminds Abraham of the paradox that we all know deep down: we need to be willing to lose it all. But once we are, we will see that we have always had everything that truly matters. The more we let go of, the closer we are to being free.

****

A monk spends many years alone, silently meditating. He sees clearly and speaks wisely. But he is far from free. Frustrated, he keeps on meditating, waiting, wondering when nirvana is going to come. It never does.

Then one day, as he walks along the road near his cave, he comes across an injured dog lying in the dirt. Kneeling down to try and help, he sees that the dog has a wound that is infested with maggots.

The monk reaches for a stick and tries to poke the maggots away. Then he realizes that by doing so, he is hurting the dog. Not only that, he is hurting the maggots too.

So he leans over, and very, very gently, starts lifting the maggots off the dog with his tongue. As he does this, the dog and the maggots dissolve into pure light, and in their place appears the Buddha, smiling at him.

****

We don't have to start by licking maggots. But that's what we're aiming for, both figuratively and maybe literally. Who says the Buddha isn't waiting for us in the form of a dying dog on the side of the road? Who says Christ isn't appearing to us as maggots or Allah in the body of a friend? Is Krishna the man begging on the corner? We know the answer: yes!

If we can take that perspective with us into the community, or even carry the possibility that there's something to it, then we've started down the road towards making every encounter sacred. Sure, we'll still act dumb sometimes. We'll hurt each other. We make mistakes. We're human as well as divine. But that's okay. We can say, "I was wrong. I hurt you." We can ask "How can I make it right?" and move on.

When we start to open to the sacred in every relationship, then we open up a whole new possibility for what the community can be. We're doing our part to turn it into a real sangha, where the game isn't to make everything look a certain way or get everyone doing what we think they should be doing, but helping us all open our minds and hearts. We can have a sangha in Bel-Air or on a street corner in Baltimore or among the monks in the Thai forest. It doesn't matter. As long as we've got food to eat (and for most of us, shelter, education, and the tools of good health are appreciated as well), we've got everything material that we need. Then it's just about love: the love that flows through us and the community.

We can't help that love. We can be grumpy, down on each other, full of anger, fear, hate. It doesn't matter. The love is always there, like the sun beyond the clouds on a rainy day. Just because we can't see it doesn't mean it hasn't always been with us. We'll see it shine through when we least expect it, when the present moment calls us to serve and we snap to, offering our help to a stranger in need.

What if all of us approach each other with the love the monk gives the dog and the maggots? It's not even a question of trying, not really, but of getting out of our own way and letting the love do its thing. Even if we fall short and get too stuck in our own knowing, we'll always get another chance. The love never stops bubbling below the surface, waiting to burst free.

Get out of the way and let it. What could our community look like then?

15

What does justice look like?

One question that is of great importance to our community: what does justice look like?

Well, since everyone is us, we're the ones who need justice. So what do we want it to look like? What sort of justice do we want for ourselves?

Sure, there's the kind of that's doled out in law courts, but we're talking about something bigger than that. Justice is really about the balance and the flow of the community. Is everyone loved? Does everyone have enough? Is everyone seen? Is everyone protected?

That's what we want, right? We want to love and be loved by those around us. We want enough. We want to have what we need to live decent lives. We want to feel like we're a part of, not cut off from. We want to be supported and safe.

So a just community, then, is one where we do our best to act from a place where we see those needs in ourselves and our neighbors. We, however imperfectly, come from a place of openness and balance and a willingness to loosen our grip on having fixed ideas of how things are or ought to be.

Part of this is making the effort. All of us are familiar with people who talk a good game and then don't deliver. We've almost certainly been those people ourselves from time to time. Our pretty beliefs aren't enough: the question is do we act justly? Do we look towards the well-being of all? Do we see us in them?

This is less of a matter of endlessly racking our brains about right and wrong and more of simply getting in touch with the needs of the present moment. Here, not-knowing is helpful. That's what letting go of our ideas is about, after all: being able to live in "I don't know."

John Rawls writes about the veil of ignorance: the idea that when we make decisions about how to shape society, we should do so imagining that we have no idea what our individual place in that society will be. If we're thinking about voting for a proposed law that, say, may hurt a specific group of people in our society, we should consider that law from a place of not-knowing. We should imagine that we ourselves might end up being in that group of people who are hurt. If we did, would we still think the law is a good idea?

The veil of ignorance is an interesting thought exercise, but from another perspective, it's also just practical advice. The Buddha tells us that our bodies just keep being reborn until we wake up from the dream of separation. Death is a part of the game (and one that we want to honor), but if we're all God, how long do we really expect God to stay dead? Ask Christ how that went, right?

That perspective can profoundly shift how we see injustice. Sure, yeah, we care, but it's easy to let things go in one ear and out the other. But if we start to consider that we ourselves may one day be born into a different body in a different place and from a different ethnicity and culture, the need for universal justice becomes less of a pretty principle and more practical self-interest. Don't we all want to feel like we'd get a fair shake if we're someone else the next time around?

Nothing lasts, remember? If we're up, we will one day be down. If we're down, we will one day be up. The wheel turns. How bumpy do we want the ride to be?

Justice is about more than intellect or principle. Can we let go enough to see what needs to be done? Can we listen enough to hear? Can we understand that when we seek to punish, we're only beating ourselves down? Can we soften?

Those of us who have power often seek to hold on to that power. Fair enough. All of us try to hold on to the things we think we need. But power, real power, is inherently just. We don't gain power by trying to take it from others or safety by walling ourselves off from the hungry. That's not power, just delusion. Real power is innate, inherent, and comes from truth. There is power in all of us because truth is within us all. The mystics say that when we speak the truth, our words have the power of law. "Let there be light," God says, and there is light, because God is speaking the truth.

God has that power. But does (he, she, unmanifested emptiness?!) try to hold on to any of it? No. Of course not. Why hold on to the river when it springs from within?

What we're pointing ourselves towards is sharing. That's the first thing we learn in school, right? But how many of us are really any good at sharing?

Well, now is a good time to learn. Our earth, our community is only growing more crowded. There is a world full of us and we all need: food, shelter, opportunity, love. Whatever we each need, we all need. Not the specifics, maybe, but the general thrust. The only way to get us all enough is through sharing.

In other words, we need to learn to share as a community. More than learn, we need to remember how to share. We know. We all know. We've just forgotten, or, more likely, we've gotten to a place where we are afraid. We're scared to let go because we think that there won't be anything left for us if we do.

Yes! There won't be anything left for us, because when we let go, we really let go, we find that we have it all. There isn't anything left for us because nothing that matters has left us.

Patanjali writes of what is called *aparigraha*, or non-possessiveness. This can also be called "no giving, no receiving." We've used that phrase before, but what does it mean here? When we exchange energy with each other, in the form of money, material goods, sex, emotions, whatever, nothing is actually being gained or lost. It's just moving around. There is no separate giver or receiver. It's all just God.

We don't get anything out of taking action because we have it all already. We're not heroes when we give money to someone in need: we're just God sharing God with God. We're not victims when we're the ones asking for help. We're just God opening to God from God. Ram Dass shares that when he looks at his guru Maharaji's journal, he sees that he has written the same thing, every day: "Ram, Ram, Ram, Ram, Ram, Ram, Ram..." That's it, day after day.

Ram, of course, means God. Our friend Ram Dass, then, is named "servant of God". His name reminds us that it is our task to open to both aspects within us. We are at once Ram and Dass.

Again, when it's all us—all Self—then none of it is personal. Whatever we think that we're giving or receiving doesn't really belong to us. Nothing is ours, individually, to share or keep. Sharing is just the natural state of energy because energy never stops moving.

When we share, we're just facilitating the natural order of things. We're balancing the books; moving energy from column A to column B. We're ending suffering by getting out of the way.

In other words, we can take the personal out of sharing and letting go and just focus our attention on what is needed in the present moment. Who needs what right now? Does God need God? Or does God need God? Yes!

If this is starting to feel silly, also yes! Adyashanti says the whole universe is just emptiness dancing. How beautiful! Love, share, let go. Don't take any of it too seriously! There is more justice in laughter than in being cold.

16

Loving the stranger

As we near the end of our journey through this book (and once we put it down and get on with the business of living), here's something curious we can pay attention to: our love for the stranger.

Many of us think of love as something to be guarded and shared only with those we trust. We need to protect our hearts, right? There is only so much love to go around, we tell ourselves, and we don't want the well to run dry.

Then one day, we find ourselves walking down the street only to come across someone in need. Normally, maybe, we look the other way, because hey, we're somebody and we've got places to go and people to see. But today, we don't.

Instead, suddenly, we find ourselves seized by a desire to help this person; not because we know them or because they have anything to offer us, but simply because we want to. In the moment, out of the blue, we are overwhelmed by an unexpected feeling of love towards a stranger. More than that, we find ourselves taking loving action. A minute ago, we were heading home, and now we're rolling up our sleeves, asking, "What can

I do for you?" and meaning it. The wall around our hearts has been breached, without warning and through no effort on our part. Far from running dry, the well has turned out to hold far more than we thought possible, and we have yet glimpsed only a hint of its true depths.

This may not happen every day (or even every month), but if we look back at our experiences or are mindful as we move forward, we will notice when it does. "Where did that come from?" we might wonder. Well, from right here, from the love inside us. Where and what else is there?

We can also ask ourselves: how many more times have we pushed away that feeling of love and the desire to help? How many times have we thought that loving a stranger would be too much to bear? More often than we might like to admit, right?

The point here isn't to feel guilty that we don't spend every waking moment offering our help to strangers in need. But by observing this sort of love when it does come up, we're getting the chance to see how universal love really is. This is a great opening to come back to non-possessiveness: our relationship with love is often governed by a sense of ownership and possession. We think our love is limited only because we believe it is something to be gained or lost; to be given or received. Love, though, like change and emptiness, just is.

This doesn't mean that most of us don't have some people we're closer to or who play bigger roles in our lives than others. But that is always a temporary state of affairs. Besides, we don't love the people we feel close to more than anybody else. We just think we do.

The love within us all, though, is enough for all of us. Limitless. When we feel the sudden urge to help a stranger in need, we get the opportunity to remember that. Seeing that, we can wonder

why we are trying to limit love and ask: do we need to?
Or are we ready to let go?

17

A call to action

We all care. We all want to do right. We all suffer. We all want to be free.

There is love and emptiness at the heart of the community. Our sangha spans the universe and takes on a billion billion different forms. We are united in our vulnerability and divine in our unity.

What choice do we have but to love it all? What can we do but say yes to the whole of the present? It's not going anywhere because we're not going anywhere.

We want things to change. Good. That's a part of what we're saying yes to. Change is a part of the whole. The emptiness can't dance without movement. When we say yes to it all, we say yes to the suffering, yes to the dark, yes to the ache in our hearts. Yes to the mud. But we also say yes to change, yes to action, yes to shining our light. Yes to the lotus.

We're on the journey to know ourselves. We can accept all of it. Take the ride. Be where we are and surrender to what is. Let go of everything we're holding on to. Share. Laugh. Not know.

Can we control ourselves or each other? No. Even if we try

really hard? No. Is any of it even ours to control in the first place? No! But that's okay, because we don't need to control anything. We don't ever have to fight reality. We are all at the mercy of the present moment and despite what we may think, it's all okay. We need only to loosen our grip and relax into the infinite love within. Is that overwhelming? Yes. But that's the point. That's what surrender is: bowing to the inevitable. Besides, there are worse things to bow to than truth and love.

That's the spirit we can bring to the community. We can be the nobody who brightens the streets we walk down. We can serve and ask for nothing in return because we know we have it all. We can be honest in our dealings with everyone we come across, search for truth in ourselves, and listen. We can make every mistake that there is to make. When we get caught up in our own righteousness, we can take a moment (or several) to laugh at ourselves, knowing we're in on the joke. We can keep practicing.

That's what we have before us: an endless opportunity to keep practicing until we wake up. Beneath all the suffering, we're an infinite group of best friends who are here to help each other see God in one another.

There is no one who isn't us. Let's act like it.

Afterword

If you enjoyed this book and want to dive in deeper, I have a few brief suggestions for where to start.

First, more books to spend time with. I had a new beginning when I read Eckhart Tolle's *The Power of Now* and *A New Earth* while spending several months in rehab for addiction and depression. Something just opened up, and I haven't been the same since. I have also been profoundly influenced by Ram Dass and his guru Maharaji (also known as Neem Karoli Baba), especially *Paths to God* and *Be Love Now*. Though I never met Ram Dass and he has passed on, he feels like a dear friend to this day.

Thich Nhat Hanh's *The Other Shore* and his translation of the Heart Sutra, Stephen Mitchell's translations of the Bhagavad Gita and the Tao Te Ching, Soygul Rinpoche's *The Tibetan Book of Living and Dying*, *Alcoholics Anonymous*, Bill Wilson's *Twelve and Twelve*, and Adyashanti's *Emptiness Dancing* are all powerful works. The teachings of Gautama Buddha, Jesus Christ, Martin Luther King, Pema Chodron, Ramana Maharshi, and Chogyam Trungpa Rinpoche also mean a great deal to me.

For anyone interested in moving beyond the page or the screen into establishing a daily spiritual practice, I would encourage making time for some sort of sitting or meditation. I like the Chan or Zen practice of silent illumination. The instructions are very simple: sit cross-legged, close your eyes, and know that you are sitting. Your body is sitting and your mind is sitting. Just sit. That's it! (For more on this practice, read Guo Gu's essay "You Are Already Enlightened". Even the title is a wonderful teaching.)

When I sit, my head starts moving fast and I feel a powerful urge to get up and do something, anything, other than keep my body still. Don't be discouraged when you experience something similar. That's part of the process. Just keep sitting. It feels like such a silly thing, but to sit is to take strong, powerful action. That's why it can be hard to do!

I also suggest cultivating at least one spiritual friendship. Find a loved one or friend who is into this stuff as well and talk about it regularly. Check in with each other, encourage each other, and don't be afraid to go far out or in deep. Have fun with it.

Finally and more broadly, I would once again suggest that all of us carry the attitude of "how can I help?" with us as we move through the world. Reach out to the people in our lives on a regular basis and ask them how they are doing. Be open to the stranger in need. Don't be afraid to take responsibility for a mess or ask how we can clean it up. But also, remember that it's all okay and all just part of our practice anyway.

Remember, too, that every part of our lives is part of our spiritual practice. Meditation, prayer, studying the Bible, the Gita, or the Koran, yes! But also everything else: work, play, friendship, family, sexuality, how we relate to one another out in the community. Beauty, ugliness, and ordinary, everyday being. None of it is left out. It's all part of the game. Accept all of it fully, sit with it, and let it go. Love all of it and all of us.

These are all just suggestions because we each have to find our own way. I often have a hard enough time walking my own road; I don't have the power to set you free too. Only you can do that.

We can appreciate the teachers who come into our lives, but we should always remember that just as no one is below us, no one is above us either. No one. If what we're doing isn't working for us, that's okay. We can always try something else. Failing and starting over may be the most constant friend and teacher of all.

But live this stuff, every day. Each one of us has the power to be the rising tide that lifts all boats. That can be our gift to each other and to the community.

Thanks for reading. It means the world to me.

About the Author

Ian Cooper lives in Los Angeles, California with his wife, Meg, and their dog, Lemon. His spiritual curiosity was nurtured first by exposure to nature, art, books, and the teachings of Jesus Christ and the Buddha. He later explored psychedelics, and has further grown through his ongoing process of recovery from addiction and soul pain. Today, he continues to study and practice and tries to walk the walk. Sometimes, he even succeeds.

You can find more of his writing at openheartbeginners-mind.com.